THANKS, NASA!

Tom Greve

Rourke
Educational Media
rourkeeducationalmedia.com

Teacher Notes available at
rem4teachers.com

www.rourkeeducationalmedia.com

PHOTO CREDITS: Cover Page: © NASA; Title Page: © NASA; Page 2, 3: © Jacom Stephens Page 4, 5: © Stanislav Pobytov; Page 6: © Library of Congress, Suljo, Andrew Ilyasov, NASA, dutch icon™; Page 8, 22 © loops7; Page 9: © jamesbenet, NASA, Dieter Spears; Page 10, 29, 41: © MARIA TOUTOUDAKI, NASA; Page 7, 11, 14, 15, 16, 17, 18, 19, 20, 21, 24, 25, 28, 30, 31, 32, 34, 35, 36, 38, 39, 40: © NASA; Page 12, 13: © oorka, NASA; Page 23, 26, 27: © NASA, Dieter Spears; Page 33: © ariwasabi, MARIA TOUTOUDAKI, NASA; Page 37: © ASSOCIATED PRESS, Photographer DR. SCOTT LIEBERMAN, NASA; Page 42: © sturti Page 43: © stocksnapper, François Pilon, Andrew Rich; Page 45: © Baris Simsek;

Edited by Precious McKenzie

Cover design by Renee Brady
Interior layout by Tara Raymo

Library of Congress Cataloging-in-Publication Data

Greve, Tom
Thanks, NASA! / Tom Greve.
ISBN 978-1-61810-120-4 (hard cover)
ISBN 978-1-61810-253-9 (soft cover)
Library of Congress Control Number: 2011945264

Rourke Educational Media
Printed in the United States of America,
North Mankato, Minnesota

rourkeeducationalmedia.com
customerservice@rourkeeducationalmedia.com • PO Box 643328 Vero Beach, Florida 32964

Table of Contents

CHAPTER ONE

Exploration: Changing Perspectives of the Earth

Humans have been exploring since the dawn of history. In fact, history itself is often marked by new findings or discoveries. Any time a person explores a place nobody has ever been to before, they increase humankind's understanding of it. This idea has propelled many of history's greatest discoveries about the physical world we call Earth.

Scientific exploration helped determine that the world is round, not flat. It also helped map Earth's continents, oceans, mountains, caves, and remote islands. Until only very recently, the greatest feats of exploration were limited to planet Earth itself.

Centuries ago, exploration was done by ships sailing across the oceans to learn how the world was laid out.

The reach of human exploration has expanded through history. This is in many ways a direct consequence of scientific advancement and improving **technology**. The **instinct** to explore has been in place since humans first contemplated a mountaintop, an ocean, or even the Moon and stars. But science has taken the will to explore and helped develop the way to reach places never before seen by human eyes.

1522
Portuguese explorer Ferdinand Magellan took three years to sail a ship around the globe, thereby demonstrating Earth is round – not flat.

1800
Invention of theodolite surveying tool allows accurate mapping of European continent.

1927
Pilot Charles Lindbergh becomes first person to fly an airplane across the Atlantic Ocean without stopping.

1953
First climbers to reach the summit of Earth's tallest mountain, Mount Everest.

1960
Submarine Trieste locates and explores Earth's greatest ocean depth.

1969
NASA puts first humans on the Moon.

Satellite technology has allowed photographic imaging of other planets and moons.

Thanks to the work of the National **Aeronautics** and Space Administration, or NASA, human exploration has increased at an **astronomical** rate in the past half century.

It wasn't until 1953 that human exploration reached the top of the world's highest mountain. Seven years later, in 1960, a manned submarine descended to the deepest point of the ocean. That meant it took all of recorded history, up to that point, for humans to reach the highest and lowest spots here on Earth. Just nine years later, in 1969, NASA explored the Moon.

Reaching the highest and lowest points on the planet were celebrated accomplishments. But they simply pale in comparison to the enormous scientific and mathematical **complexity** of trying to rocket people beyond the pull of Earth's **gravity**, account for the lack of oxygen and extreme cold of outer space, and land on the Moon.

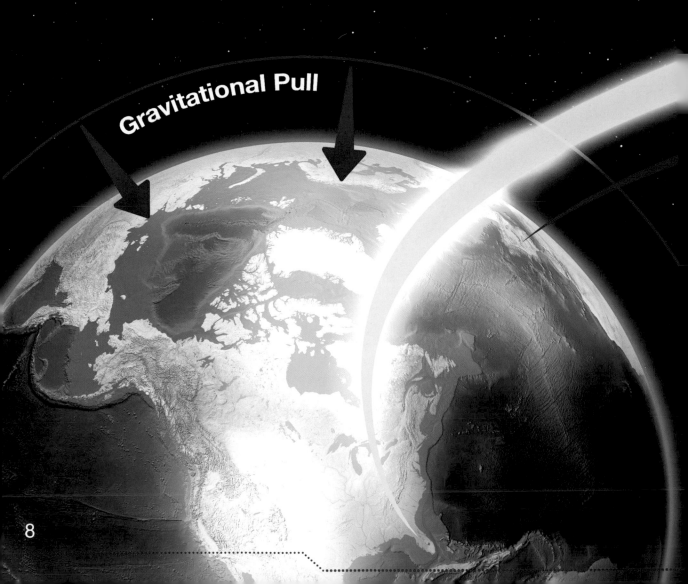

Gravitational Pull

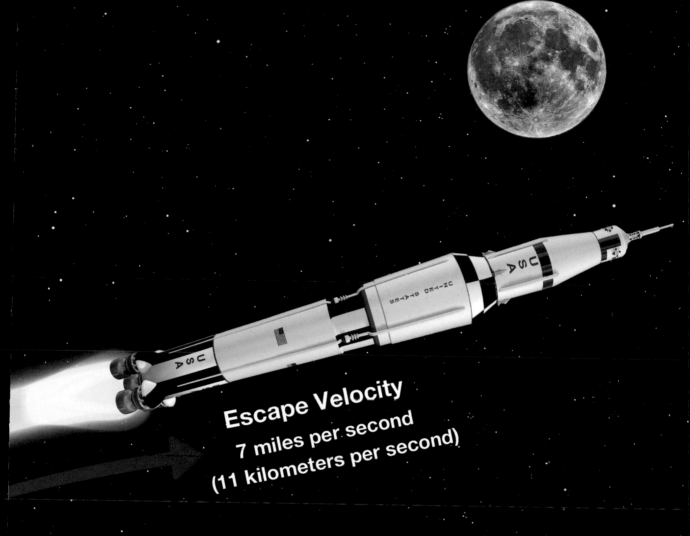

Escape Velocity
7 miles per second
(11 kilometers per second)

No person or group in history has changed humankind's perspective of Earth more than NASA. Thanks to NASA and its scientific work over the past half century, humans have stepped outside the confines of their own planet. They not only explored outer space and the Moon, but witnessed Earth as it truly is: a living blue orb floating in the cold darkness of outer space.

CHAPTER TWO

NASA and a Mandate for the Moon

NASA was created as an agency of the United States federal government in 1958 by President Dwight Eisenhower. Its work spearheads American research into space travel and exploration. Its creation was motivated in large part by the politics of the **Cold War** between the United States and Russia.

THE SPACE RACE:

*In 1957, Russia – known then as the Soviet Union – successfully launched a **spacecraft** called Sputnik into orbit, thereby beating the U.S. into space. Four years later, Russian Yuri Gagarin became the first human to fly into space. U.S. efforts geared up to not only match Russia's space exploration, but exceed it.*

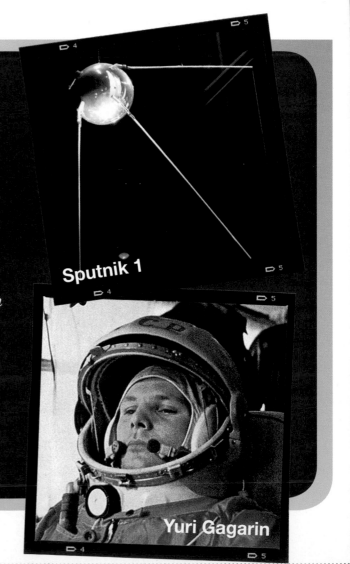

Sputnik 1

Yuri Gagarin

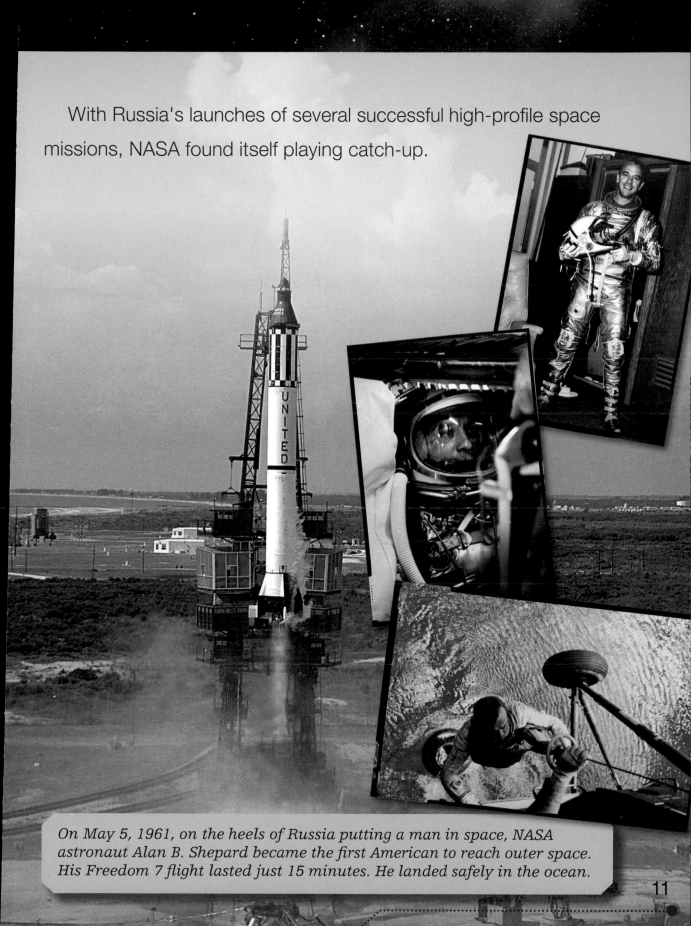

With Russia's launches of several successful high-profile space missions, NASA found itself playing catch-up.

On May 5, 1961, on the heels of Russia putting a man in space, NASA astronaut Alan B. Shepard became the first American to reach outer space. His Freedom 7 flight lasted just 15 minutes. He landed safely in the ocean.

Less than a month after Shepard's flight, President Eisenhower's successor, President John F. Kennedy, boldly told Congress and the nation that he wanted an American to explore the surface of the Moon and return safely to Earth by the end of the decade. This directive focused much of NASA's work through the 1960's, and firmly placed the U.S. at the forefront of the space race with Russia.

John F. Kennedy

Although Cold War politics may have motivated President Kennedy and NASA to put an American on the Moon, it was science that made it possible.

NASA KNOWLEDGE:

*Much of what NASA's early scientists knew about rockets had come thanks to the work done decades earlier by Robert Goddard. Considered the father of modern rocket science, Goddard constructed and tested the first rocket using liquid fuel in 1926. Although he was largely dismissed by the scientific community during his lifetime, his contributions to the physics of rocket **propulsion** are now considered revolutionary. NASA's test flight facility in Maryland is named the Goddard Space Flight Center in his honor.*

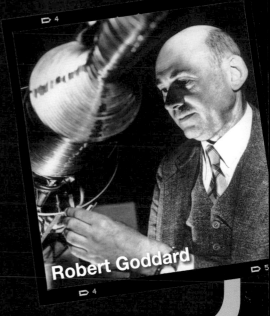

Robert Goddard

As a scientific research organization, NASA's accomplishments come through extensive theorizing based on past observations and research. Then scientists use **experimentation** to test those theories. Finally, scientists put what is learned into subsequent experiments. The rocket science required for space travel evolved over many decades with each breakthrough built on earlier successes and failures.

In addition to countless teams of scientists, researchers, physicists, mathematicians, chemists, and rocket scientists working within NASA itself, thousands of others from private companies and universities were involved in the work to reach the Moon. These outside technicians and scientists continue to aid NASA in many capacities.

The research and design of a spaceship to carry someone to another **celestial** body was unlike any feat of engineering ever attempted before. But as NASA began work on Apollo, communication and cooperation between far-flung factions of its scientific and engineering teams became difficult to organize.

The push to reach the Moon was expensive and labor-intensive. In 1960, NASA had about 10,000 employees. By 1966, that number more than tripled to 36,000 workers.

NASA's space flight headquarters is in Houston, Texas. It's also home to the astronaut training center. In 1973, it was renamed in honor of former President Lyndon Johnson, who was in the White House from 1963 until early 1969.

Since 1968 all NASA space flights have launched from The Kennedy Space Center at Florida's Cape Canaveral. It is named in honor of former President Kennedy.

15

NASA used managers from the U.S. military to oversee all aspects of the Apollo project in an effort to organize the complex multi-site effort, and to meet the **lunar** landing deadline of January 1, 1970.

NASA KNOWLEDGE:

The Crossroads of Science, Politics, and the Military

NASA's chief administrator from 1961 until 1968, James Webb, is credited with navigating NASA through the lead-up to the Apollo Moon landing. His work included maintaining NASA's relationship with political leaders in order to secure continued funding through the turbulent months and years following President Kennedy's assassination in 1963. He also selected Air Force Major General Samuel Phillips to serve as the centralized authority over the many scientific teams working on Apollo. Phillips' organizational work was instrumental in keeping the Apollo mission on track.

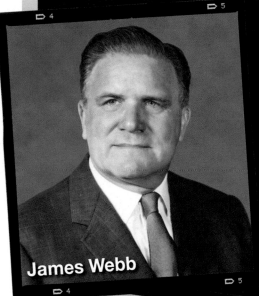

James Webb

Samuel Phillips

Dr. Wernher von Braun

NASA's leading rocket scientist over its first decade of existence was Dr. Wernher von Braun. Ironically, he had previously worked against the U.S. when he designed rockets for the Nazi party in Germany during the lead-up to World War II. Throughout his career as a scientist, he frequently reverted to propulsion and **aerodynamic** concepts originally put forth by Robert Goddard more than a half-century earlier.

17

Most of NASA's numerous factions of scientific teams work outside of the spotlight in labs, offices, or testing facilities. The spacecrafts and rockets are usually built by outside companies hired and supervised by NASA.

But NASA's astronauts are the public face of the organization. They represent a whole new breed of American heroes. Their work is highly technical and incredibly dangerous. They are modern day explorers of the great unknown, carrying the imagination of the public with them.

NASA KNOWLEDGE:

For its first space missions NASA only considered men for service as astronauts. Astronauts had to be less than 5 feet 10 inches tall (1.78 meters) because of the tight quarters inside spacecrafts.

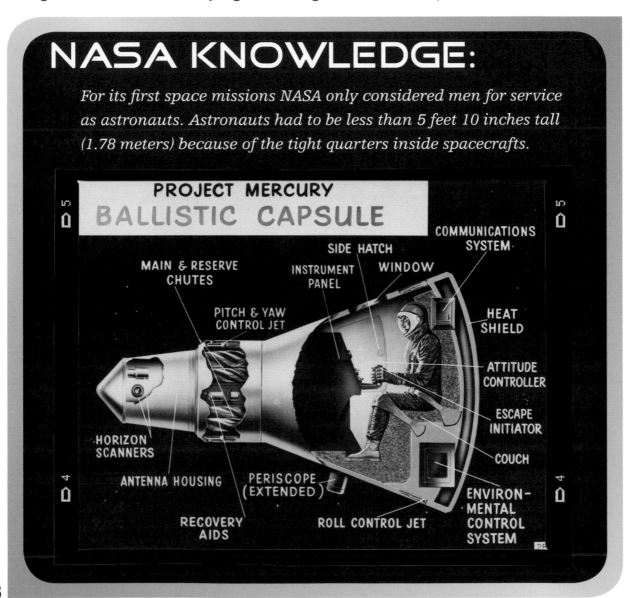

PROJECT MERCURY
BALLISTIC CAPSULE

COMMUNICATIONS SYSTEM

SIDE HATCH

MAIN & RESERVE CHUTES

INSTRUMENT PANEL

WINDOW

PITCH & YAW CONTROL JET

HEAT SHIELD

ATTITUDE CONTROLLER

ESCAPE INITIATOR

HORIZON SCANNERS

COUCH

ANTENNA HOUSING

PERISCOPE (EXTENDED)

ENVIRON-MENTAL CONTROL SYSTEM

RECOVERY AIDS

ROLL CONTROL JET

RECOVERY AIDS

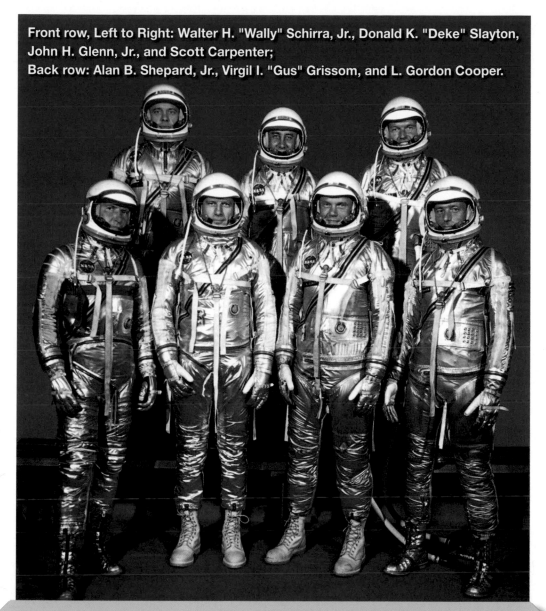

Front row, Left to Right: Walter H. "Wally" Schirra, Jr., Donald K. "Deke" Slayton, John H. Glenn, Jr., and Scott Carpenter;
Back row: Alan B. Shepard, Jr., Virgil I. "Gus" Grissom, and L. Gordon Cooper.

The original seven served NASA in many groundbreaking early space missions, all building toward an eventual lunar landing. To this day, less than 400 individuals have been chosen to serve as NASA astronauts. By the 1980's, women and minorities were also selected as astronauts.

The first U.S. astronauts were selected in 1959 before the mission to the Moon or any manned space flight had begun. NASA asked for a list of pilots from the U.S. military who met specific qualifications relative to experience, scientific **aptitude**, and physical size. After stringent testing, NASA picked seven astronauts now known as NASA's original seven.

The 1960s marked many firsts for NASA's manned space flight program as it worked to meet President Kennedy's stated national goal of a Moon landing before the end of the decade.

Less than a year after Alan Shepard's brief flight into space, NASA's reach into the heavens expanded with Astronaut John Glenn rocketing into orbit around the Earth. His Friendship 7 spacecraft made three trips around the planet. After four and a half hours, he re-entered Earth's atmosphere and splashed down in the Atlantic Ocean. This was hailed as a major breakthrough by NASA.

NASA KNOWLEDGE:

John Glenn, from Astronaut, to Senator, and back again.

One of NASA's original 7, Ohio native John Glenn had studied math in college before joining the military during World War II. He became an accomplished fighter pilot before his selection as an astronaut. His 1962 flight into orbit around the Earth put the U.S. on equal footing with Russia in the space race.

Twelve years after his first space flight into orbit, John Glenn was elected to the U.S. Senate from his home state of Ohio. He became the oldest person in space in 1998 when, as a 77-year-old astronaut, he was a crewmember onboard the space shuttle Discovery.

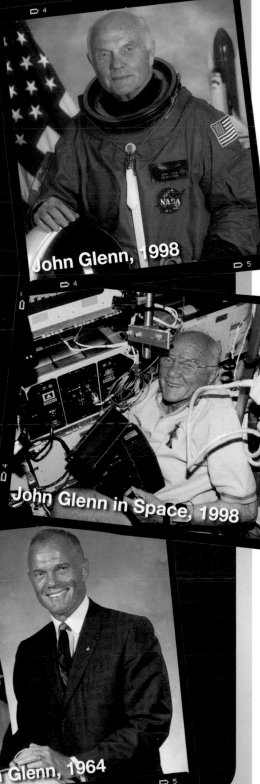

John Glenn, 1998

John Glenn in Space, 1998

John Glenn, 1962

John Glenn, 1964

Not every NASA project leading up to Apollo was a success. As is the case in many scientific endeavors, some of NASA's experiments along the way created more questions than answers about the trip to the Moon. This meant scientists had to reevaluate equipment, procedures, and the even the **physics** of how to get from point A, or Earth, to point B, the Moon.

LUNAR ORBIT RENDEZVOUZ

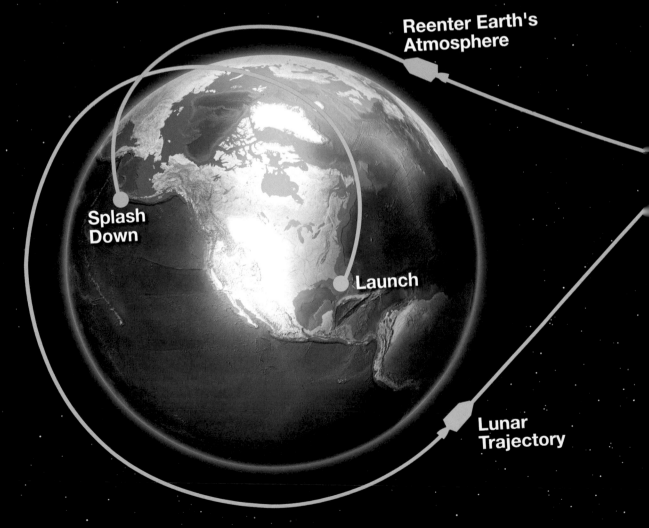

Reenter Earth's Atmosphere

Splash Down

Launch

Lunar Trajectory

A tragic reminder of how dangerous, deadly, and unpredictable NASA's work can be happened in January of 1967 when a fire broke out on Apollo 1 as it readied for launch on a test flight. Three astronauts died including Gus Grissom, who'd been one of NASA's original 7. The disaster cast temporary public doubt on the mission to the Moon.

Virgil "Gus" Grissom, Edward White, and Roger Chaffee

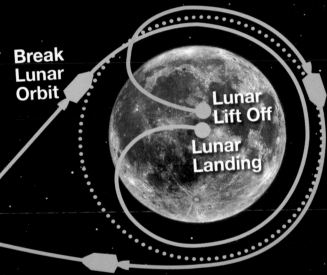

Break Lunar Orbit

Lunar Orbit Rendezvous

Lunar Lift Off

Lunar Landing

Return to Earth

After years of conceptual research, scientific testing, and mathematical theorizing, NASA scientists reached agreement on their strategy to actually land on the Moon. The lunar orbit **rendezvous** plan meant a launch rocket would send a small command ship with an attached lunar landing craft into space and into orbit around the Moon. The lunar lander would then lift off from the Moon's surface and reunite with the command ship still in orbit. Once the astronauts were back on the command ship, the lunar landing craft would be ejected into outer space. The command module would return to Earth and land safely in the ocean where the U.S. Navy would retrieve the spacecraft and the astronauts.

CHAPTER THREE

Mankind's Giant Leap to a New Perspective

By July of 1969, eleven years after NASA's formation and eight years after President Kennedy's call to explore of the Moon, Apollo 11, was ready for launch.

On July 16, the Apollo spacecraft, consisting of the command module called Columbia, and the lunar landing module called Eagle, were ready. They were mounted on NASA's 363 foot-tall (110.642 meter) Saturn V launch rocket at the Kennedy Space Center.

The Saturn V rocket used to launch Apollo 11 remains the largest and most powerful rocket booster ever built by the United States.

A three person crew consisting of astronauts Neil Armstrong, Edwin "Buzz" Aldrin, and Michael Collins were at the controls inside Apollo's command module.

At about 9:30 a.m., Apollo 11 blasted off into space. Thousands of NASA scientists, technicians, designers, engineers, and millions of people watching television, waited intently to see if this mission would be a success.

Armstrong, Collins, and Aldrin had all been on previous space flights before NASA assigned them to the Apollo 11 mission.

Four days after launch, while in orbit around the Moon, Neil Armstrong and Buzz Aldrin climbed from the command ship into the Eagle, or lunar landing module, and began their decent toward the Moon's surface. Collins remained in the command ship.

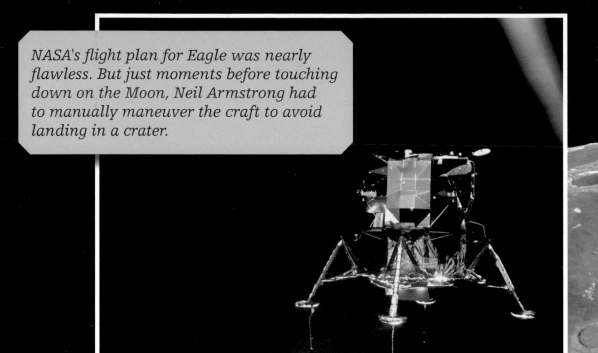

NASA's flight plan for Eagle was nearly flawless. But just moments before touching down on the Moon, Neil Armstrong had to manually maneuver the craft to avoid landing in a crater.

NASA KNOWLEDGE:

Houston Mission Control

All NASA space flights are in radio contact with the launch control room at the Kennedy Space Center leading up to, and during, space launches. Once they leave Earth's atmosphere, their ground contact switches to mission control inside the Johnson Space Center in Houston. That is why astronauts begin their radio conversations with the word "Houston".

On July 20, 1969, the Eagle landed on the Moon. Astronaut Neil Armstrong set up a TV camera and captured live footage of his exit out of the lunar module. With more than 600 million people watching the grainy images on television, he stepped onto the Moon's surface. A short time later he was joined by Aldrin.

With his first step onto the Moon's dusty surface, Neil Armstrong uttered the phrase now associated with the Apollo mission and NASA's work up to that point: "That's one small step for man, one giant leap for mankind."

NASA's successful exploration of the Moon not only meant humankind's reach had extended beyond Earth, it also gave every human a greater sense of perspective on planet Earth itself. Images taken by the Apollo crew showing the Earth floating in the night sky gave millions of humans pause to consider their planet as they'd never seen it before. It remains among the most important moments in American history. It is arguably the most celebrated accomplishment of science, innovation, and technology in the history of exploration.

The first Moon landing lasted about 21 hours, some of which Armstrong and Aldrin spent sleeping inside the Eagle.

NASA KNOWLEDGE:

The astronauts collected Moon rock samples to bring back to Earth for study. They conducted scientific experiments while on the Moon and left a small plaque reading: *"HERE MEN FROM THE PLANET EARTH FIRST SET FOOT UPON THE MOON JULY 1969 A.D. WE CAME IN PEACE FOR ALL MANKIND."*

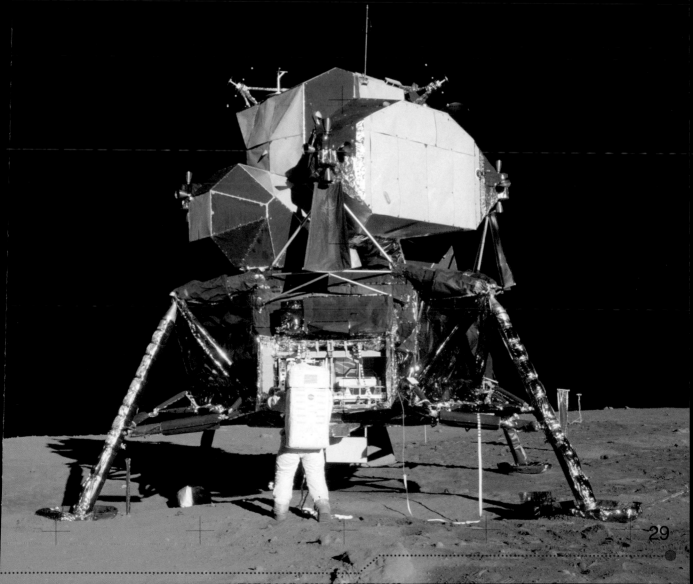

Armstrong and Aldrin flew the Eagle to its reunion with the command module and returned safely to Earth on July 24, 1969. The crew received a hero's welcome.

In the minds of most Americans, Apollo 11 was, and remains, NASA's finest hour. It was a scientific triumph of research, engineering, organization, and execution.

NASA's Apollo 17 was the last human exploration mission to the Moon. Using a space-age dune buggy called a lunar rover, the crew traveled further, and collected more surface samples, than any previous mission. Commanding astronaut Eugene Cernan remains the last human being to have stood on the Moon.

In all, there have been just 12 humans, all NASA astronauts, who have actually stood on the Moon. The scientific knowledge gained from these missions has greatly advanced human understanding of the solar system. The technological expertise of the mission has impacted everyday life in the ways we communicate using things like cellular phones and wireless Internet connections. But the cultural effect of the mission may have been an enhancement of public understanding about our own planet.

If a person never left their house, they wouldn't truly know what it looked like from the outside. Similarly, NASA's exploration of space, and in particular its manned missions to the Moon, gave every human being a view of their planetary house from the house next door.

"We went to explore
the Moon, and in fact
discovered the Earth."
—Eugene Cernan,
NASA astronaut

Less than a year after Apollo 11's lunar exploration, the first Earth Day was organized and celebrated.

Jaw-dropping images of Earth taken from the Moon by Apollo 11 inspired more popular awareness of environmental issues like pollution control and recycling. This is one part of NASA's legacy of changing the perspective of our own planet. It's a legacy that continues to this very day.

NASA KNOWLEDGE:

One of NASA's key scientific roles in recent years has become monitoring Earth's atmosphere and protective ozone. NASA's observation of apparent ozone depletion and its affect on global climate change could become Earth's most pressing scientific concern.

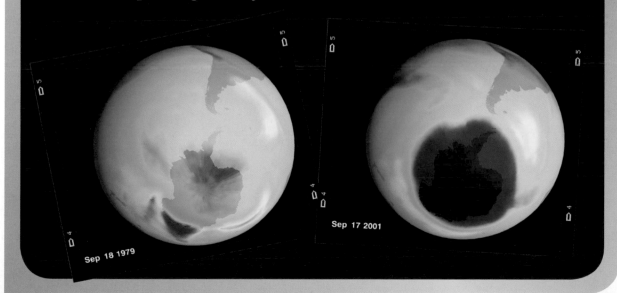

Sep 18 1979

Sep 17 2001

CHAPTER FOUR

NASA Changes Focus: The Shuttle Era and Beyond

With Apollo missions ending in 1972, NASA's next directive was to develop and launch a reusable spacecraft known as the space shuttle.

Like Apollo before it, nearly a decade's worth of design, engineering, production, and experimentation went into trying to perfect the space shuttle. Between the first flight in 1981 and the final flight in the summer of 2011, NASA flew 135 shuttle missions into space.

Columbia launch for 1981 maiden mission

Five shuttles: Atlantis, Challenger, Columbia, Discovery, and Endeavor, were built for the program. They could each be used to carry satellites into orbit, then rendezvous with the same satellites on subsequent missions to perform service or repair.

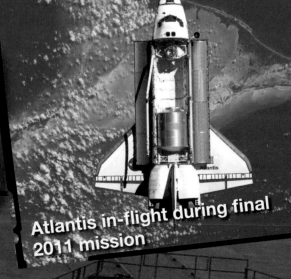

Atlantis in-flight during final 2011 mission

NASA KNOWLEDGE:

During the shuttle era, NASA added its first female and African-American astronauts. Sally Ride, a physicist from California, became the first American woman, and youngest person, ever in space when she was a crewmember onboard a 1983 space shuttle Challenger flight.

On the very next Challenger flight later that same year, Guion Bluford, Jr., a former Air Force pilot from Pennsylvania, became the first African-American in space.

Sally Ride

Guion Bluford, Jr.

> *Hubble has produced some of the clearest images ever made of the universe's most distant objects.*

Among NASA's shuttle mission triumphs was the 1990 launch of the Hubble telescope into orbit around Earth via the space shuttle Atlantis. The powerful space telescope has been repaired or upgraded five times since it began transmitting images in 1993. It is expected to continue transmitting images until 2014. Hubble observations have led to breakthroughs in **astrophysics**.

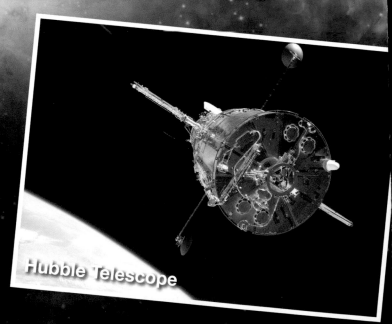

Hubble Telescope

NASA experienced its two worst disasters during the space shuttle era. Both Challenger and Columbia were lost to in-flight complications that resulted in the destruction of both spacecraft and the deaths of 14 astronauts.

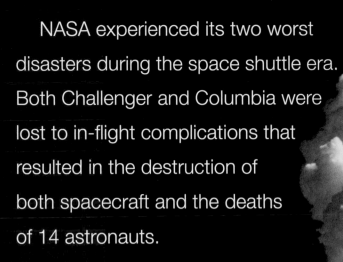

NASA and its space shuttle program were dealt a severe blow in January of 1986 when the space shuttle Challenger exploded just seconds after launch. The shuttle itself disintegrated over the Atlantic Ocean. All seven astronauts onboard, five men and two women, including teacher Christa McAuliffe, died.

Seventeen years later, in February of 2003, the shuttle Columbia broke apart while re-entering Earth's atmosphere minutes before its scheduled landing. Debris scattered across Texas and Louisiana. Columbia's seven person crew, which again included five men and two women, died.

Despite these setbacks, and criticism related to cost, the space shuttle program played a vital role in furthering space exploration and in the establishment of the International Space Station.

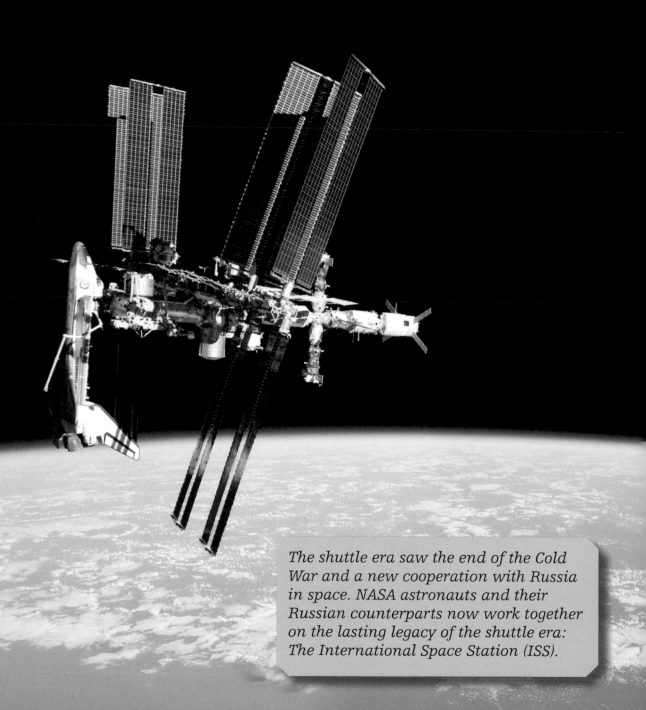

The shuttle era saw the end of the Cold War and a new cooperation with Russia in space. NASA astronauts and their Russian counterparts now work together on the lasting legacy of the shuttle era: The International Space Station (ISS).

The last space shuttle launched from Florida on July 8, 2011. When Atlantis landed on July 21, 2011, it marked the end of the space shuttle program. NASA astronauts will continue work at the International Space Station. The station is equipped with six laboratories to research medicine, technology, and space science. The American astronauts will be transported home by Russian vessels.

NASA hopes private aerospace companies will one day transport astronauts and offer commercial cargo shuttle service to the space station. Until then, NASA astronauts will travel back and forth to the station on Russian spacecraft.

One research function being studied at the ISS is the long-term effects of zero-gravity exposure on the human body. NASA hopes this research will have **implications** for future manned spaceflights to Mars, which would require more than a year in transit.

Since NASA's beginning, astronauts have had to perform intense training exercises in zero-gravity conditions to simulate conditions in space.

*NASA scientists have even observed what appear to be rivers of liquid on Saturn's largest moon, Titan. Satellite images reveal the rivers flow with liquid **methane** instead of water. Other than Earth, it is the only known evidence of surface liquid anywhere in the solar system.*

NASA's observational reach now extends far beyond the limits of human space flight. Newer, far-reaching probes have provided NASA with precise data on the surface of Mars and other corners of the solar system.

Human spaceflight to other planets remains a possibility only in theory. But unmanned spacecraft like the Mars rovers Spirit and Opportunity have documented traces of water in soil samples from Mars. Although Mars is almost certainly lifeless, the water traces are the best indicator that life could have once existed on Mars.

CHAPTER FIVE

Nifty NASA:
Technology We Can All Use

Beyond providing humans with a new perspective on Earth, NASA has made massive contributions to society in terms of technology. Space exploration has spurred technological advances in **aviation**, **telecommunication**, computers, robotics, and medicine.

While cell phones and wireless computer networking are part of today's information age, much of the technology was already in use by NASA as they worked on the Moon landing.

Some projects are designed by NASA. Other times they partner with other companies to work on a specific application for space travel. NASA calls the result a spinoff.

NASA KNOWLEDGE:

NASA scientists created temper foam in the 1960's to create better cushions for astronauts and pilots to sit on during flight. That technology is now used in everything from mattresses to padding on the inside of football helmets.

When NASA needed a way to keep items from floating away from astronauts in the zero-gravity conditions of space, they used a Swedish company's simple, non-liquid adhesive. Today this material is used widely throughout the world. It's commonly known as Velcro.

Since the Apollo era, millions of people have been walking in the astronauts' shoes, so to speak. Lightweight spacesuit designs developed by NASA are now commonplace in gym shoe manufacturing.

CHAPTER SIX

Politics and Science

Whether extending human reach into space or working to create new technologies, NASA is a scientific research organization under the influence of the nation's ever-changing political climate. NASA's funding and its directives are shaped by politics, and as a result, can sometimes change.

NASA KNOWLEDGE:

Program funding by year

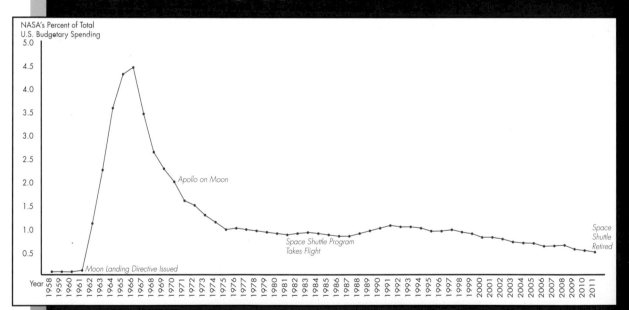

NASA's budget has been near or below 1 percent of the nation's overall annual budget every year since 1973. Its all-time high for annual funding was in 1966 during research and development of the Apollo Moon landing missions. The Moon landings came at the end of NASA's greatest period of political, and as a result, financial support.

While NASA's intense scientific work in space exploration has greatly enhanced our understanding of what's out there beyond our own planet, NASA's most important function may well be its legacy of changing the perspective humans have of life on our own planet.

Glossary

aerodynamic (AIR-oh-dye-NAM-ik): designed to move through air easily, with minimum resistance

aeronautics (air-uh-NAW-tiks): the science and practice of designing, building, and fixing aircraft

aptitude (AP-ti-tood): natural ability to do something well

astronomical (ass-truh-NOM-uh-kuhl): having to do with the stars, planets, and space; very large

astrophysics (ASS-tro-fiz-iks): the science of the physical properties of the universe

aviation (ay-vee-AY-shuhn): the science of building and flying aircraft

celestial (suh-LESS-chuhl): having to do with the sky or heavens

Cold War (KOHLD WOR): competitive struggle between nations not involving armed conflict

complexity (kuhm-PLEKS-eh-tee): the status of having many parts or being complicated

experimentation (ek-SPER-uh-mehn-TAY-shuhn): scientific testing to prove or disprove a theory

gravity (GRAV-uh-tee): the force that pulls objects toward Earth's surface and keeps them from floating off into space

implications (im-pluh-KAY-shunz): the meaning or significance of something as it relates to something else

instinct (IN-stingkt): behavior that is displayed naturally, not learned

lunar (LOO-ner): having to do with the Moon

methane (METH-ane): a colorless, odorless gas

physics (FIZ-iks): the science that deals with matter and energy, including the study of light, heat, sound, motion, and force

propulsion (pruh-PUHL-shuhn): the force by which a plane or rocket is pushed along

rendezvous (RON-day-voo): an appointment to meet at a certain time and place

spacecraft (SPAYSS-kraft): a vehicle that travels or is used in space

technology (tek-NOL-uh-jee): the use of science and engineering to perform practical tasks

telecommunication (tel-uh-kuh-myoo-nuh-KAY-shuhn): the science dealing with the sending and receiving of messages over long distances by telephone, satellite, radio, or other electronic means

Index

Websites to Visit

www.spacecenter.org

www.nasm.si.edu/exhibitions/attm/a11.om.1.html

www.science.nationalgeographic.com/science/space

About the Author

Tom Greve lives in Chicago with his wife Meg and their two children, Madison and William. He loves to escape the city lights and contemplate the Moon and stars in the night sky while imagining what it would be like to be an astronaut.

Ask The Author!
www.rem4students.com